Copyright © 2005 by Mary F. Pecci

All rights reserved.
No part of this book may be reproduced
without written consent of the author.

First Edition
ISBN 978-0-943220-15-4

Distributed by:
PECCI EDUCATIONAL PUBLISHERS
www.onlinereadingteacher.com
sales@onlinereadingteacher.com

Other Books by Mary F. Pecci
At Last! A Reading Method for EVERY Child! - NEW SIMPLIFIED EDITION
At Last! A Reading Method for EVERY Child! - READING SPECIALIST EDITION
Why Johnny Ain't Never Gonna Read (A Challenge to the Nation)
How to Discipline Your Class for Joyful Teaching
5 Steps to Save Our Schools

Pecci Reading Series
Pre-Primer I
Pre-Primer II
Pre-Primer III
Primer
1^1 Reader

Super Spelling
Book One

Super Seatwork
Letter-Recognition
Color Words
Number Words
Content Areas
Phonic Grab Bag
Linguistic Exercises
Word Skills

This Pre-Primer is designed to be used in conjunction with:
At Last! A Reading Method for EVERY Child!

ACKNOWLEDGMENTS

This reading series is dedicated to my beloved brother, Dr. Ernest F. Pecci, and his remarkable daughter, Diana Pecci La Brecque, who set this project into motion by saying those magic words, "Yes! You CAN do it!"

Sincere appreciation also goes to my sister, Marguerite Pecci Kelley, for her story suggestions and for always being on call to backboard ideas.

And a very special thanks goes to June Triesch, quintessential Kindergarten teacher, who retired on her 80th birthday, about whom such teachers it has been written, "God doesn't have hands; He uses the teacher's hands," for her constant faithfulness over the years as dearest friend and mentor.

Teacher's Guide

Pages 61 - 64

Vocabulary Word List - p. 61

Word-for-Word Dialogue
between Teacher and Student - p. 62 - 64

In this reader, 25 words are formally introduced. However, reading vocabulary will not be limited to these 25 words because students will be acquiring independent decoding skills as they progress through this reader. This reader serves only as a springboard, from which students will be able to read *any* material on (and in most cases above) their academic level.

Hi, I am Carlos.

This is my 🏐 ball.
It is fun to play with.

I want to play 🏐 ball.
I want to play 🏐 ball.

It is fun!
It is fun!

Hi, I am Anna.

See my 🩰.

I want to get on my 🩰.

Look at this!
It is fun to do this.
It is fun!
It is fun!

The Big 🪁

Look Carlos.
Look at my 🪁 go up.
My big 🪁 can go up, up, up.

This is fun.
It is fun to play with a 🪁 .

Oh, oh, Anna!
I see the 🪁 come down.
Down, down, down.

Help, Carlos!
Help me with my 🪁.
Help! Help! Help!

Now the 🪁 is in the 🌳.
Help, Carlos, help!

I can help you, Anna.
I can help you get the 🪁.

See me go up and down.
Up and down to the 🪁.

Oh, Carlos!
You did help me get my 🪁 .
Now we can play with it.

You are fun to play with, Carlos.
You are fun to play with too, Anna.
Carlos and Anna are fun to play with.

We Play ⚽ Ball

Look at that boy, Sam.
He can play ⚽ ball.
Look at that boy play!

We want to play ⚽ ball too.
We can play with that boy.

Hi, I am Sam.
Hi, I am John.
This is my dog, Bo Bo.
We want to play ball with you.

Hi, I am Carlos.
You can play ball with me.

Look at this.
You can do it too.
Run to the 🐾 ball.

Get the 🐾 ball in the 🥅 .
Run, run, run!
You can do it too.

Go, Sam, go! You can do it!

Oh, Oh, Look at Bo Bo.
Bo Bo can not play with us.
He is not a boy.
He is a dog.
A boy can play ⚽ ball.
A dog can not play ⚽ ball.

The 🥏

Look at me, Anna.
I have a 🥏 .
I am a big boy.
See me do this.

Can I play with it, Carlos?
I want to play with a boy, Anna.
I want to play with a boy.

Look, Carlos,
I see Sam.
Sam is a boy.
He can play 🥏 with you.

Look, Sam.
I have a 🥏 .
Can you play it with me?

Look at us play 🥏, Anna.
I am a big boy.
Sam is a big boy.
See us play with a 🥏.

Oh, oh!
Look at the 🥏 go in the 🪟.
Oh, my! Oh, my!

Anna! Did you do this?
I did not do it.
A boy did it.

Is the boy Carlos?
He is not with you.
Is the boy Sam?
He is not with you.
Did Carlos and Sam run, run, run?

Anna and Pam

Hi! I am Anna.
Hi! I am Pam.

Will you play with me, Pam?
We will have fun.

Can you come to my 🏠 , Anna?
Come with me, Pam, and we will see.

Can I go to Pam's 🏠 ?
I want to play with Pam.
We want to have fun.

You can go to Pam's 🏠 .
Have fun with Pam.
I will come to get you.

See my 🪑 🪑, Anna?
This is for you.
This is for me.

See my ☕☕, Anna?
This is for you.
This is for me.

See my ◎ ◎, Anna?
This is for you.
This is for me.

Oh, oh!
And this is my pet cat, Scratch.
This is *not* for you, Scratch.

Get down, Scratch.
You can not play with me and Anna.
You can not play with us now.

Go, Scratch go!

The 🔍🔍

Oh, Ken!
Look at the 🔍🔍.
I want to have a 🔍.

I see the 🔍🔍, Carlos.
I want to have a 🔍 too.
I will get a 🔍, Ken.
I will get a 🔍 too, Carlos.

Look, Pam.
Carlos and Ken have 🍭🍭.
We want to have a 🍭 too, Pam.

Carlos will get a 🍭 for you.
Ken will get a 🍭 for me.
Carlos and Ken will help us.

We do not want to get up now.
We want to play with the 🎈🎈.
Come and get a 🎈.

We can not come now.
Pam and I are in the 🏊.
Will you help us?

Look at the 🍭🍭 come to us!
A 🍭 for me, Pam.
A 🍭 for you, Anna.

You did help us, Carlos and Ken.
And you did not have to get up.
See the 🍭🍭 come to us!

Carlos and the

Oh, my!
Carlos can not play the 🎤.
Tell him not to play it.
That boy can not play the 🎤.

I have to go now, Anna.
Tell him not to play that 🎤.

Carlos! Do you have to play that  ?

I want to play it for you.
I want to play it for Pam.
Tell her to come in.

I will play it for you.
I will play it for her.
Tell her to come in.

Tell him I do not want to come in.

I do not want him to play that .

Oh, look, Pam. Look at the dog and the ball.

Look at the ball go up and down!

Oh! See that ball go!
Look at Carlos!
Look at him now.
Now he can not play that 🎤.

The dog did it for you.
The dog did it for me.
The dog did it for us!

The Little 🦷

Look at my little 🦷, John.
It is just a little 🦷.
It will not come off.

I want it to come off.
I want a big 🦷 to come in.
Can you help me?

It will go up an down, Carlos.
It will not come off.

I can help you.
I will have to get my dog.

You do not want just a little 🦷.
You want a big 🦷 to come in.

I will help you, Carlos.
I will do this to the little .

Come, Bo Bo, come.
I will do this to you.

Now run, Bo Bo, run!
You have to run, run, run!

Look, Carlos.
See the little 🪁 come off!
Now a big 🪁 will come in.
My dog did help you.

The Little Ball

Look at my little ball, Ken.
I can get it in the .

That is just a little ball.
You can not get it in the , Carlos.
You have to have a big ball.

That boy can not get the ball in the .
It is just a little ball, Ken.
Tell him it is just a little ball.

Tell her I CAN do it.
I will do it for you.
I will do it for me.
I will do it for us.

Oh! Just look at that boy now!

Tell him it is in the , Meg.
Tell her the little ball is in the , Ken.

I did it for you.
I did it for me.
I did it for us!

Anna Can Help

Look at that girl, Meg.
Look at her go up!
She can do that on 🥾.

I want to do it, Meg.
I want to do it too, Kim.
We can have fun with that girl.

Hi, I am Kim.
Hi, I am Meg.
Can you help us to do that?

Hi, I am Anna.
I can help you to do it.
You can do it too.

Look at me do it.
Jump up and go!
Go, girl, go!
Go, girl, go!

Look at her go!
She can do it. We can do it too.

Oh, oh! You are down.
To jump on , you have to
DO it and DO it and DO it!

Oh, oh! Just get up and go, go, go!
You have to DO it and DO it and DO it!
Go, girl, go! Go, girl, go!

You DID it, Kim! You DID it, Meg!
Go, girl, go! Go, girl, go!
Now you can have fun with me!

Ken Can Help

"I will get this for my little girl," said Mother.
"She will want this.
 It is for Meg.
 It is for her.

"I will get that for my little boy," said Mother.
"He will want that.
 It is for Ken.
 It is for him."

"Oh, my," said Mother.
"I have to have help with this big 🛍.
I do not have my car with me.

"I see a little 🍐 go down.
I see a little 🍌 go down.
I see a little 🍎 go down.

"I have to have help with this big 🛍."

"I see my mother with the big 🛍," said Ken.
"She will have to have help.
My little car can help her.

"Go little car, go!
Go little car, go!
We have to help Mother.
I will tell Mother we can help her."

"Look at my big boy in the little car,"
said Mother.
"Just look at him.
He can help me with the big 🛍.

"He is not my little boy now.
He is my big boy now.
Just look at him help me.
He can help me with the little car.

The 🪧

"Look at my little pet dog," said Kim.

He wants to get on the 🪧 with me.

"Come, Bo Bo, come. You can get on the 🪧 with me.

"Look at him, Anna,
He wants to go up and down."

"We have to have help now," said Kim.
"Will you help us, Anna?
Will you help us get up on the ⌄__⌄ ?

"My little pet dog wants to go up on the ⌄__⌄ .
Look at him. He wants to go up.
He wants to go up, up, up."

"I will help you get up," said Anna.
"I will help you get up."

"Oh, oh! Look at my little pet dog!" said Kim.

"He wants to get off the ⌴.
 Help! Help!"

"Mother is at the ▯ ," said Anna.
"I will tell her to help us.

"Help, Mother, help!
 The little dog is off the ⌴ !"

"Look at Mother!" said Anna.
"Look at Mother!
She *did* help Bo Bo.
See Bo Bo jump on Mother!"

Mother said, "Now, Anna and Kim,
a ⌣ is for a little girl.
a ⌣ is for a little boy.
a ⌣ is NOT for a little dog."

Fun in the 〰️

"Just look at that 〰️," said Anna.
"Do you want to swim in the 〰️?"

"I do want to swim in the 〰️,"
said Meg. "It is fun to swim."

"Come, Meg," said Anna.
"We will swim in the 〰️.
Run with me to the 〰️."

"This is fun," said Anna.
"Look at me swim in the 〰️.
Come and swim with me."

"It is fun to jump up and down in
the 〰️ too," said Meg.
"Look at me jump up and down in
the 〰️."

"This is fun!" said Anna.
"This is fun!" said Meg.

"Oh, my!" said Anna.
"Do you see that?
I see a big, big fish."

"Help!" said Meg.
"I do see that big, big fish.
It will get us!"

"Help! Help! Help!
Run! Run! Run!" said Anna and Meg.

"Look at Anna," said Carlos.
"Just look at that girl run!"

"Look at Meg," said Ken.
"Just look at that girl run, too!"

"It is fun to play with this big, big, fish," said Carlos.

"This is funny!" said Ken and Carlos.

The 🏰

"Father," said Kim, "will you help me?
I want to have fun with a 🏰.
Will you do it for me?"

"I will help my little girl," said Father.
"I will do it for you.
I have to have the 🪣 and the 🥄.
Now, we will have fun."

"Look at this, my little girl," said Father.
"Look at this 🏰 go up, up, up!"

"Oh, Father," said Kim.
"I will have fun with this 🏰.
You can help me.
Just look at it go up, up, up."

"This is fun," said Father.
"This is fun," said Kim.

"Oh, oh!" said Kim.
"Look at that big, big 🌊.
 Father, it will come and get my 🏰.
 Help, Father, help!"

"Run, Kim, run!" said Father.
"That big 🌊 will come in on the 🏰.
 Now it will go down, down, down.
 Run, Kim, run!"

"Oh, look, Father," said Kim.
"This is funny.
 Now we do not have a 🏖 .
 Now we have a fish.
 It is just a little fish.
 See him swim in my 🪣 ."

"Oh, Kim," said Father.
"I see the little fish.
 That is funny."

Fun with Mother and Father

"It is fun to play with Father," said Anna.
"Look at him get the little car to go."

"It is fun to play with Mother, too," said Carlos.
"She will get her little car to go now."

"We have a little car, too," said Anna.
"Mother and Father are fun to play with.
Just look at us!"

"Oh, oh," said Father.
"I see the cat play with the 🐟, the 🐟 with the fish on it."

"I do not want her to do that," said Mother.
"The 🐟 will jump up at her."

"Go, cat, go," said Father.
"Do not play with that 🐟.
Do not play with that 🐟."

Did the cat go?
The cat did *not* go.
Oh, oh! Look at the 🎁 jump up!

"Oh, my!" said Mother.
"See that 🎁 jump up!
Father did tell the cat not to play with the 🎁 .
Look at that cat now.
Just look at her fur.
Her fur is up, up, up!"

"Help! Help!" said Father.
"Help! Help!" said Mother.
"Help! Help!" said Anna.
"Help! Help!" said Carlos.

"Look at that cat jump!" said Anna.
"Get that cat off!" said Carlos.
"We can not play with that cat on this," said Father.

"Just look at us now!" said Mother.

Pre-Primer III
Vocabulary Word List

Pages 1 - 4
p. 1 - Carlos
p. 2 - It
p. 3 - Anna

Pages 5 - 8
p. 6 - me
7 - you

Pages 9 - 12
p. 9 - boy (**oy**) *
He
p. 12 - us

Pages 13 - 16
p. 13 - have

Pages 17 - 20
p. 17 - will
18 - Pam's
p. 19 - for

Pages 21 - 24
(Absorption Story)

Pages 25 - 28
p. 25 - tell
him
p. 26 - her (**er**)**

Pages 29 - 32
p. 29 - little
just

Pages 33 - 36
(Absorption Story)

Pages 37 - 40
p. 37 - girl (**ir**) ***
she

Pages 41 - 44
p. 41 - said
Mother

Pages 45 - 48
(Absorption Story)

Pages 49 - 52
p. 49 - swim
p. 51 - fish
p. 52 - funny (**Y on end**) ****

Pages 53 - 56
p. 53 - Father

Pages 57 - 60
p. 59 - fur (**ur**) *****

* Introduce the "**oy**" Sight Family beforehand.

** Introduce the "**er**" Sight Family beforehand.

*** Introduce the "ir" Sight Family beforehand.

**** Introduce "**Y**" on the <u>end</u> says "**E**" beforehand.

***** Introduce the "**ur**" Sight Family beforehand.

Word-for-Word Dialogue

Reminder:

> 1. Write a list of the words to be introduced that day for the assigned pages, as illustrated on p. 99-101 in *At Last!*.
>
> 2. Introduce the words as scripted below.
>
> 3. Review the Word List as per the NOTE on top of p. 112 of *At Last!*.
>
> 4. Put the words introduced on flashcards and review them each day *before* introducing new words. (No word cards are needed after the Pre-Primers.)
>
> 5. Reinforce words with the Word Reinforcement activities on p. 135-140 in *At Last!* and apply the Pre-Requisite skills reinforcement activities to words.

Now, you are ready to begin!

Following is the word-for-word dialogue between teacher and student for introducing every word in this reader:

Pages 1 - 4

	Teacher:	**Student:**
Carlos -	This boy's name is "Carlos." What's the clue?	C a r l o s
It -	I am looking at - What's the clue?	I t I t

(**Note:** As a general rule, it is advisable to introduce both the capital and lower-case forms of each word, when applicable. Ex. It, it.)

Anna -	This girl's name is "Anna." What's the clue?	A n n a

Pages 5 - 8

me -	One for you and one for - What's the clue?	m e m e
you -	One for me and one for - What's the clue?	y o u y o u

Pages 9 - 12

NOTE: Introduce the Sight Family "oy" during the Phonic Period before introducing the word "boy."

	Teacher:	**Student:**
boy -	Underline O-Y. What's the Sight family? What's the word?	b o̲ y̲ o y b o y
He -	This word is "He," as in "H̲e̲ is a boy." What's the clue?	H e̲
us -	He will do it for - What's the clue?	u s u̲ s̲

Pages 13 - 16

have -	How many crayons do you - What's the clue?	h a v e h̲ a̲ v̲ e

Pages 17 - 20

will -	Will you like this story? Yes, you - What's the clue?	w i l l w̲ i l̲ l̲
Pam -	We had this word before. Can you read it?	P a m
Pam's -	When something belongs to someone, we add **'s**. Underline the **'s**. What's the word?	 P a m '̲s̲ P a m ' s
for -	I wonder who this package is - What's the clue?	f o r f̲ o̲ r̲
	(**Note**: Exaggerate a long "o" sound to assist decoding.)	

Pages 21 - 24 - (Absorption Story)

Pages 25 - 28

tell -	If it's a secret, you shouldn't - What's the clue?	t e l l t e̲ l̲ l̲
him -	One is for her and one is for - What's the clue?	h i m h̲ i̲ m̲

NOTE: Introduce the Sight Family "er" during the Phonic Period before introducing the word "her."

her -	Underline E-R. What's the Sight family? What's the word?	h e̲ r̲ e r h e r

Pages 29 - 32

little -	If it's not big, it might be - What's the clue?	l i t t l e l̲ i̲ t̲ t̲ l̲ e

	Teacher:	**Student:**
just -	This word is "just," as in "It is <u>just</u> a little tooth." What's the clue?	j u s t j <u>u s t</u>

Pages 33 - 36 - (Absorption Story)
<u>Pages 37 - 40</u>

NOTE: Introduce the Sight Family "**ir**" <u>during</u> <u>the</u> <u>Phonic</u> <u>Period</u> before introducing the word "girl."

girl -	This is not a boy. It is a - What's the clue?	g i r l <u>g</u> <u>ir</u> <u>l</u>
she -	A boy is a "he," and a girl is a - What's the clue?	s h e <u>s</u> <u>h</u> <u>e</u>

<u>Pages 41 - 44</u>

said -	I heard every word you - What's the clue?	s a i d <u>s</u> a i <u>d</u>
Mother -	Who will pick you up today, your father or your - What's the clue?	M o t h e r M <u>o</u> <u>th</u> <u>e</u> <u>r</u>

<u>Pages 45 - 48</u> - (Absorption Story)
<u>Pages 49 - 52</u>

swim -	A little fish can - What's the clue?	s w i m <u>s</u> w <u>i</u> m
fish -	The boys and girls can swim like a - What's the clue?	f i s h f <u>i</u> <u>s h</u>

NOTE: Introduce "**Y**" on the <u>end</u> says "**E**" before introducing the word "funny."

funny -	Clowns make us laugh because they are so - What's the clue? Yes, "**Y**" on the end says "**E**."	f u n n y f <u>u</u> <u>n n</u> <u>y</u>

<u>Pages 53 - 56</u>

Father -	Who will pick you up tonight, your mother or your - What's the clue?	F a t h e r F <u>a</u> <u>t h</u> <u>e r</u>

<u>Pages 57 - 60</u>

NOTE: Introduce the Sight Family "**ur**" before introducing the word "fur."

fur -	Underline U-R. What's the Sight family? What's the word?	f <u>u r</u> u r f u r